THE STATUE OF LIBERTY

AMERICAN SYMBOLS

Lynda Sorensen

The Rourke Book Company, Inc.
Vero Beach, Florida 32964

PHOTO CREDITS
All photos courtesy of National Park Service (pages 4 and 17 by
Brian Feeney; page 8 by Richard Frear)

Library of Congress Cataloging-in-Publication Data

Sorensen, Lynda, 1953–
    The Statue of Liberty / by Lynda Sorensen
        p. cm. — (American symbols)
    Includes index.
    ISBN 1-55916-046-2
    1. Statue of Liberty (New York, N.Y.)—Juvenile literature.
2. Statue of Liberty National Monument (New York, N.Y.)—Juvenile
literature. 3. New York (N.Y.)—Buildings, structures etc.—Juvenile
literature. [1. Statue of Liberty (New York, N.Y.) 2. National
monuments. 3. Statues.]
I. Series.
F128.64.L6S65 1994
974.7'1—dc20   94–7052
                                                               CIP
Printed in the USA   AC

TABLE OF CONTENTS

THE STATUE OF LIBERTY

A tall, metal lady stands on Liberty Island in New York Harbor. Her official name is *Liberty Enlightening the World*. She is much better known as the Statue of Liberty.

For more than 100 years the statue has been a **symbol** of **liberty**, or freedom, in America.

In her raised right hand, Miss Liberty holds a welcome lamp. Her left hand holds a lawbook dated July 4, 1776. That was the day a few bold Americans signed the Declaration of Independence from England.

The Statue of Liberty holds a torch of welcome in her raised right hand

A GIFT FROM FRANCE

A French professor, Édouard de Laboulaye, suggested that France present the United States with a huge statue. The French felt a bond of friendship with the United States. They had become free people, like the Americans, in the late 1700's.

The statue was planned as a gift to honor the 100th birthday of the United States in 1886.

A French **sculptor**, Frederic Auguste Bartholdi, crafted the statue's copper "skin." Alexandre Gustave Eiffel, the builder of France's famous Eiffel Tower, built the steel "skeleton" of the Statue of Liberty.

The Statue of Liberty was a gift to the United States from France

LIBERTY CROSSES THE ATLANTIC

Bartholdi completed the Statue of Liberty in Paris, France, in 1884. Each part of the statue was marked and taken apart for shipment to America. The copper skin and iron frame were packed in 214 boxes. They were shipped across the Atlantic Ocean to New York.

The statue was rebuilt and placed on a tall **pedestal**, or platform, built of concrete and granite rock. A ceremony on October 28, 1886, celebrated the statue's completion.

The Statue of Liberty rises from a pedestal on Liberty Island, New York City

THE LONG, TALL LADY

The Statue of Liberty rises 305 feet from the bottom of her pedestal to the tip of her torch. She is about the height of a 23-story building, or a football field standing on end. Including the pedestal, she is the world's tallest statue.

Liberty's right arm stretches 42 feet. The statue's nose alone is four feet, six inches long. Move over, Pinocchio!

The mighty Statue of Liberty stands under a shower of fireworks

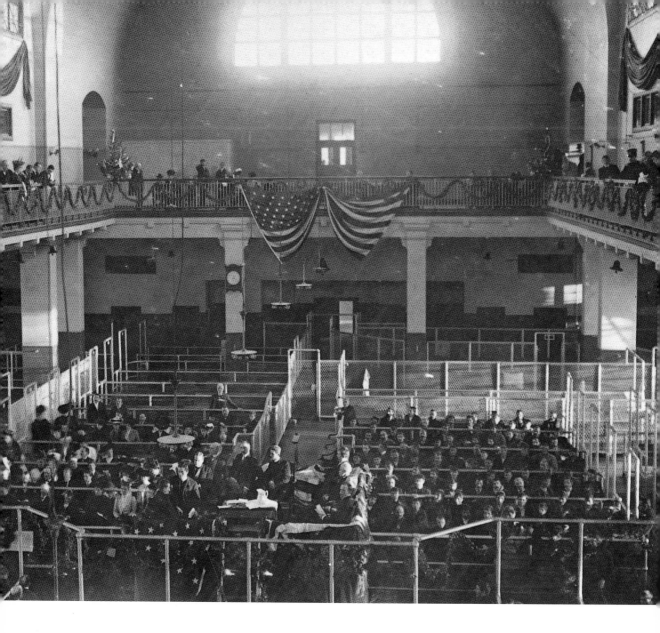

Immigrants being checked at the Ellis Island Immigration Station in the early 1900's

Entry to the Ellis Island Immigration Museum

THE QUEEN OF ELLIS ISLAND

After the Statue of Liberty was completed, millions of **immigrants** arrived in New York. Immigrants are people who leave their home country to live in another.

Immigrants arrived in New York by ship. They were taken to a station on Ellis Island, less than one-half mile from Liberty Island.

One of the first sights for immigrants as they neared their new home was the towering Statue of Liberty. For many of the newcomers the statue became a lifelong symbol of freedom.

Immigrants were taken to a processing station on Ellis Island, a short distance from the Statue of Liberty

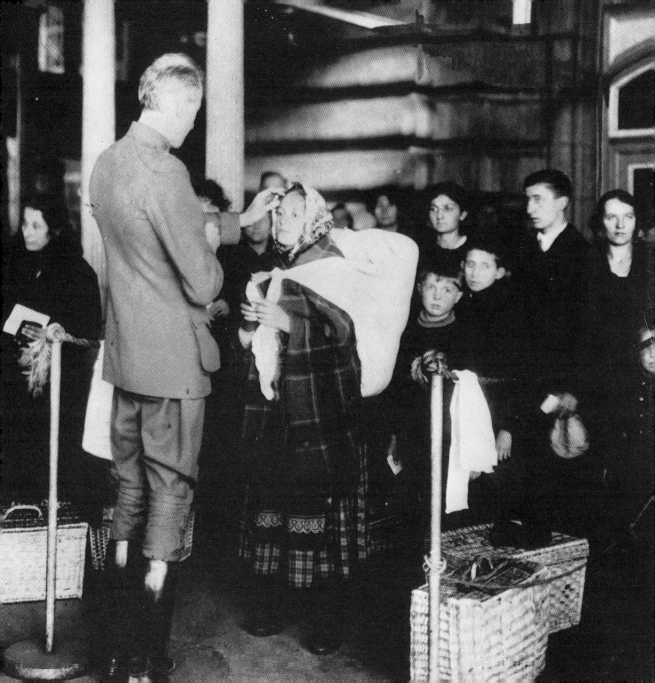

A NATIONAL MONUMENT

The Statue of Liberty became a national monument in 1924. National monuments are certain places or structures with important natural or historical value. They are protected and cared for by the National Park Service of the United States.

The Statue of Liberty and the old immigration station on Ellis Island make up the Statue of Liberty National Monument. The monument also includes the American Museum of Immigration at the base of the statue.

The old immigration station on Ellis Island is part of the Statue of Liberty National Monument

THE LADY TAKES A BATH

After nearly 100 years, the Statue of Liberty showed signs of old age.

The National Park Service began cleaning and repairing the statue in 1983. People in France and the United States raised money for the project.

The Statue's copper skin was cleaned inside and out. The torch and viewing platform in the crown were rebuilt.

By her 100th birthday on July 4, 1986, the aging lady no longer showed her age.

By her 100th birthday, July 4, 1986, the Statue of Liberty had been made youthful again

VISITING THE STATUE OF LIBERTY

Millions of people visit the Statue of Liberty each year. They reach the statue by taking a one and one-half mile ferry boat ride from New York City.

An elevator and long stairway lead up through the pedestal. People who continue upward into the statue itself must climb a stairway. The stairway in the statue rises 142 steps into a viewing area in Liberty's crown. On a clear day the view of New York City is breathtaking.

A viewing area is located in Liberty's crown

A SYMBOL OF FREEDOM

A broken chain lies at the Statue of Liberty's feet. The chain stands for the right of people to be free, not chained.

The statue in the harbor has a special meaning for millions. American immigrants remember the statue for the feeling of hope it gave them.

Millions of other Americans, returning from trips overseas, remember the Statue of Liberty, too. She welcomed them back home.

Glossary

immigrants (IHM uh grintz) — people who leave one country and move to another

liberty (LIH bur tee) — freedom

pedestal (PEH dus tul) — a platform or base on which something, such as a statue, can be set

sculptor (SKULP tor) — an artist who carves works of art from rock, clay or some other material

symbol (SIM bull) — something which stands for something else, as a flag stands for a country

INDEX